Understanding and sensitively raising highly sensitive children

How to accompany and support your emotional child on their journey and raise them happily without scolding them

Mareike Waldecker

CONTENTS

What you can expect in this book

There are many things to watch out for when raising children. The course is set for life. This responsibility in particular means that raising a child is not always an easy task. Parents know that the defiant phase is exhausting, but also important.

When a child is going through a developmental spurt, it can be nerve-wracking. But here, too, you know that this is important and it will pass. But what if the child is always very sensitive and reacts to things with a lot of emotions, perhaps having even less control over their feelings than another child? The environment usually judges our entire behavior, often after just a few minutes and impressions. The child is "too shy" or "too hyper", a highly sensitive child might be told. It is possible that they have been told from an early age that they are not okay the way they are, that their personality is not okay. So how can they develop a personality with healthy self-esteem and acceptance of themselves?

As parents, you can not only act as a bridge between society and your child, but also give your child a basis of basic confidence and self-esteem.

In order to create a good foundation for your child, this book provides a few tips and tricks for support options and crisis prevention. In order to fundamentally strengthen the understanding between parents and child in both directions, the theoretical background is presented. This will enable you to better understand what is going on in your child, but also to explain this to your child so that they understand themselves and you.

In addition, the potential of high sensitivity should also be presented, because there is nothing wrong with emotions in the first place and you can definitely find ways to use this potential.

What does high sensitivity mean?

PROFESSIONAL CRITERIA FOR HIGH SENSITIVITY AND CURRENT RESEARCH FINDINGS

People with high sensitivity perceive more stimuli than people with normal sensitivity, which is also visible in examinations of brain areas. These above-average or more intense stimuli can quickly make them feel overwhelmed. They occasionally feel at the mercy of the stimuli and helpless in the situation. It affects 15 to 20% of the population, so it is more widespread than you might think.

We all absorb stimuli and also have individual ways of perceiving them. However, while normal-sensitive people are sometimes quite unimpressed by a certain level of stimuli, a highly sensitive person may already have reached or even exceeded the limit of overstimulation. Psychotherapist Dr. Elaine Aron coined the term "Highly Sensitive Person" (HSP) in 1996. She began counseling highly sensitive people at an early stage and conducting research in this field.

High sensitivity does not manifest itself in the same way in all those affected. As it is only one characteristic of our personality, those affected remain individuals. Just because they have the trait does not define their entire character and personality.

Basically, the differences can be divided into sensing, feeling and thinking, although many people are sensitive in several areas.

Sensory-sensitive people react particularly to sounds, smells, light or colors. These people have highly developed senses. This often results in talents in creative areas. Due to the many sensory impressions in everyday life, they may feel overloaded by these impressions more quickly or be particularly sensitive to noise, for example.

Emotionally sensitive people, on the other hand, usually focus particularly on interpersonal matters. They are particularly compassionate and helpful.

Their challenge is also not to feel overwhelmed by what they perceive on an emotional level. The vibrations and interpersonal perceptions are often more extreme and more important to them than the spoken words.

Cognitively sensitive people have the need to categorize facts into right and wrong and think in complex contexts. Their talents often lie in scientific or technical areas. Problems could arise if their complex thinking hinders communication in their everyday life.

The majority of people with high sensitivity tend to live somewhat withdrawn lives and are introverted. However, this does not mean that they do not want to have contact with other people. They are often just as integrated into circles of friends as people without high sensitivity. At the same time, there are also highly sensitive people who are more extroverted. These people are often not yet aware that they are highly sensitive. This is why they often suffer from excessive demands that they cannot explain.

It is important to know and internalize that high sensitivity is not an illness or disorder. It is now seen as a predisposition, just like body size or eye color. Highly sensitive people just need to be careful in their everyday lives that they don't become overwhelmed, as this can happen to them more quickly. However, researcher Dr. Elaine Aron has found that people with high sensitivity are more frequently affected by a mental disorder. This means that they need to be much more mindful of themselves and their emotions in everyday life in order to prevent this in the best possible way.

SPECIAL FEATURES FOR CHILDREN

For children, all stimuli are initially new and therefore challenging. However, a normally sensitive child learns to deal with them quickly. A highly sensitive child needs longer to do this and can feel overwhelmed by the stimuli more quickly. However, they also perceive these stimuli in a more differentiated way. They therefore take in more, even less important information. Because the child absorbs so many stimuli, they have to carry out a much more strenuous evaluation.

Funnily enough, high sensitivity is more socially accepted in adults than in children. For adults, for example, it is considered conscientious and responsible if you think about your answers for longer. With children, for example at school, this is immediately judged negatively. The child has not learned, is less intelligent or less capable, is a common conclusion. However, due to their high sensitivity, they may need a little more time to think because they have to absorb and process a lot more stimuli than a normally sensitive child. When adults are more reserved in their contact with new people, they are seen as thoughtful and deliberate. Children, on the other hand, are seen as too shy or as having social anxiety. Society is merciless with children, they are judged very harshly. With adults, we recognize the individuality and diversity of people and demand tolerance towards minorities. With children, on the other hand, we want to talk them into our own way of doing things. Because children are not yet able to "control" their emotions so well, they are seen as "exhausting" or "crybabies". With adults, we would find such assessments offensive and disrespectful. But isn't it the same with our children?

Children with high sensitivity who are judged in an environment that is not sensitive to high sensitivity are often seen as too shy. In situations of excessive demands, however, they are also considered to be unrestrained in their emotions. However, these assessments do not actually reflect the personality or the characteristics of high sensitivity, but are merely the effects of the wrong way of dealing with them. They often feel misunderstood or not understood at all by those around them. They therefore often see themselves as lone warriors. Children do not yet have any real influence on their own lives, they are determined by others. If an adult feels overwhelmed at work or in their free time due to too many stimuli and impressions, they can explain these circumstances and take time out by leaving the room. A child cannot simply leave the classroom, as this would be seen as disobedient. In the same way, children have no influence on changes if we adults don't let them. So involve your children according to their age. In childhood, it is much easier for us to influence these important characteristics. We can lay the foundations for ensuring that emotions are not a taboo subject and that our children learn to accept and love themselves.

HOW CAN I RECOGNIZE THAT MY CHILD IS HIGHLY SENSITIVE?

In general, of course, it must be said that there are generally common characteristics of high sensitivity, but this does not mean that every child or adult displays all or the same characteristics. Ultimately, they are still independent people with their own personality. They should not be generalized and defined solely by this characteristic.

High sensitivity can be particularly evident in children's sensory experiences. They may be more sensitive in their sense of touch, sense of balance, sense of sight, sense of hearing, sense of taste and/or sense of smell. If you notice a particularly large number of examples in your child, this may indicate high sensitivity.

Examples of sensitive abnormalities:

Sense of touch: sensitive to certain materials, touching others, dirty hands and face, strong temperature fluctuations

Balance: sensitive to fast movements, activities with no ground contact; avoidance of prone position as a baby; omission of crawling and crawling; anxiety during movement

Sense of sight, sense of hearing: sensitive to noises and movements even in infancy; overstrained when watching television; distracted by noise and bright colors; good perception of very quiet noises

Sense of taste and smell: sensitive to intense smells and tastes, temperature of the food, carbon dioxide, mushy consistency; "picky eater"

Conspicuous behavior would also be if your child does not like change and is always interested in the same toys. This refers to an above-average level, i.e. it cannot be excited or distracted by something new. It is not only new things that often cause anxiety. Does your child often play alone, feel insecure in groups and react with crying or aggression? These can also be signs. However, high sensitivity also has many great characteristics, such as the ability to reflect, empathy, conscientiousness and many more.

This special sensitivity often affects not only the emotional world, but also the body. It can react more sensitively to touch and, according to current research, also has an increased likelihood of allergies.

You don't have to immediately notice that someone is highly sensitive; there are those affected whose emotional world is particularly strong on the inside, but who make a very introverted impression on the outside.

If you suspect that your child is highly sensitive, there are now various online tests that have been created by scientists. However, care must always be taken here, as this is of course a self-diagnosis. As it is not an illness or disorder, it is not generally dangerous to carry out such tests. However, mental disorders etc. sometimes have similar symptoms and may then go unnoticed. It is therefore advisable to consult a therapist if you suspect you have a disorder. It should also be borne in mind that, in principle, no examination is necessary if there is no psychological distress.

POSITIVE ASPECTS OF HIGH SENSITIVITY - IS IT ALL A QUESTION OF PERSPECTIVE?

The scientific knowledge that high sensitivity is not a disease or disorder makes it easier to shed light on the positive aspects. The characteristics of high sensitivity include a high capacity for empathy, the ability to reflect, conscientiousness and the demands placed on oneself. If you look at these characteristics and don't talk about them in the context of high sensitivity, then you wouldn't assume that they are negative traits. And that is exactly what we are talking about here.

A highly sensitive person, whether child or adult, often possesses these great qualities and many more that we or our society would even classify as positive. Of course, they are often more pronounced in highly sensitive people and this sometimes makes it overwhelming, especially for those affected, but these characteristics can also be seen as potential and positive. Just because something or someone deviates from the "norm" does not necessarily mean it is bad. Everyday life can be difficult for the person affected, but with practice and, above all, a change of perspective, this can be seen as an incredible opportunity. Above all, it is important not to approach them with the idea that they are ill. In principle, they want to be treated in the same way as everyone else and, above all, not looked at with pity or not taken seriously.

As people with high sensitivity often have a very good ability to reflect, they can not only assess their thoughts and actions well, but also influence them. And it is precisely from this that a particular strength can emerge. Many people spend years working on personal development for this particular strength and still find it difficult.

However, it is important with this potential that there is no internal pressure to perform. It is always important to be good as it is at the moment. The ability to reflect enables a good and realistic assessment of your own personality and actions, which is why you should not be overly self-critical. Trusting that you can assess things correctly is important if you want to be happy with yourself in the long term and accept yourself as you are. And that also means that not every day is like the next, and that's okay.

Comparisons with other children increase the pressure to conform and the feeling of not being good enough. Therefore, try to give your child the feeling that it is always okay to be the way they are. Even if you take this for granted, it often fades into the background in our busy everyday lives. And highly sensitive children in particular sense this and have an increased need for it.

What does my child need from me?

UNCONDITIONAL LOVE AND COMMUNICATION AS THE BASIS

What does unconditional love mean?

A parent's love must not be tied to any conditions, it must be unconditional. It nourishes our entire path through life. It can determine our future relationships, but it can also create a suitable learning environment in infancy and early childhood.

Ultimately, we want to rely on our parents to always be there when we need them. Basically like our base that we can always come back to, in a value-free space.

Basically, your child first and foremost needs you as a parent. By just being there, you are already doing a lot right. Quality rather than quantity is important here. Don't just be there physically, but also mentally and above all with your heart. Your baby or child will sense when this is not the case. Assuming that all parents love their child and want the best for him/her, the basic attitude of the primary caregiver is crucial. You send messages to your child, whether you want to or not, whether you say it or not. Children notice very early on whether love and acceptance are conditional or whether we accept them unconditionally. Phrases such as "If you are good ..." or "If you are nice ..." do not suggest unconditional love, but that the child must behave appropriately in order to receive your approval.

A highly sensitive child often has the feeling of being out of order and different from everyone else. As parents, you should try to counteract this. They should feel that no matter what happens or how they feel, their parents are always there and won't judge them. A highly sensitive child in particular senses when you wish they were different, even if you don't say so. You can create the basis for later trust in infancy and toddlerhood.

It is important to say at this point that this unconditional love and acceptance has nothing to do with spoiling or a lack of consistency.

Talk to your child and listen to them. Through open communication, you can learn a lot from your child about what they need. However, treat them like a child and only expect them to make decisions that are not too much for them. Be there when they need you and take them seriously. If they need you as a parent in a crisis situation, be there.

Take the emotions seriously and try not to reassure, but to comfort. Calming creates the impression that the feelings should go away quickly and "It's not that bad ..." or "You don't need to be afraid ...". Consoling, on the other hand, means simply being there and absorbing the emotions "I'm here, it's okay that you're sad. You are not alone ...".

The basic building block should be a trusting relationship between you and your child. This is not always easy and as a parent you often get little feedback and recognition. A normally sensitive child can usually be reassured by their parents, which tells them that they are doing a good job and they become more confident. A highly sensitive child is often not so easy to reassure and therefore lacks the confirmation that they are doing the right thing. This insecurity usually also contributes to a poorer relationship with your child. So be confident in what you do. Listen to your gut feeling.

A highly sensitive child will initially need a lot of attention and encouragement. However, if you live with the predisposition of "high sensitivity" and simply allow it to be part of your life, then not only you but also your child will be able to recognize the special potential. Recognize and accept the special needs and invest in the future.

Be sensitive to your child's needs, but also to your own. It is good for your child to be close to you, to feel safe and calm, which is reassuring. Everyday life can be very exhausting and exhausting for your child, but also for you. Take breaks so that you can recharge your energy tank. And if that means leaving the household chores to be done during nap time, then so be it. And that's okay. Set the right priorities for yourself. It's no good for you or your child if you're exhausted and drained.

Always remember that you know your child best. Listen to your intuition, to your gut feeling. A guide is only ever a medium to give you suggestions. You have to do things your own way, because your child will also notice if you are not being authentic and it will be even more stressful for you. And if you really feel you need expert advice, don't be afraid to ask for support.

How can we communicate with understanding?
Communication is often the key to many things. We need to ask ourselves how we want to talk and interact with our children. Think about what scolding and shouting triggers in you and what this must then trigger in a small child who is being shouted at by their caregiver.

Scientists have also found that we do not get our children to change their behavior by shouting and scolding, at least not in the long term. In some cases, it is even seen as a form of psychological violence. We also want our children to become self-confident and strong personalities. How would you like to be spoken to and dealt with? You can ask yourself that again and again.

In communication, the term active listening is used time and again. By actively listening, you are also signaling "I understand you and am actively taking the time to be with you now ...". This also works in a crisis situation, i.e. when your child is crying desperately. Try to accept it and put up with it for the time being.

This shows that these feelings are okay. This does not mean that you should sit in front of your child and watch them cry. The point is that you first allow it to happen and don't want to immediately calm it down and find a solution. Read again in the previous chapter about the difference between calming and comforting, as the child may not even know what is going on and will not be able to give you an answer. Mirror what you perceive "You seem sad, don't you?" or "You're really angry right now, aren't you?" The child will let you know if you are right. Express your suspicions, even if you are not sure. This lets your child know that you are concerned. If a solution is needed, one can be sought after a short time. Sometimes, however, it is enough for the child to get rid of their emotions and for the caregiver to simply catch them and understand them. There is an incredible amount of specialist literature on active listening that is easily accessible. It's worth reading up further. The use of non-violent communication can also be helpful. It requires some practice, but even parts of it can be supportive. You can find out more about this on the Internet or at a counseling center. You can learn to better recognize and accept needs and fears. You can also find lots of exercises and explanations on the internet.

So now the child is crying and screaming and you are angry and stressed because he has done something wrong. How do you react?

Accept the anger and sadness and signal this: "I notice that you are angry or sad right now...". You can still comfort them. But then explain in the form of an I-message what has upset you "I was upset because we made an agreement and you didn't keep it ...". This is different from "You didn't ... again ...".

However, this only works if the child is in a responsive state. If the situation has already escalated to such an extent that your child is trying to exert power or similar (hitting, insulting, etc.), clear boundaries are needed. A consequence may follow, but this must never consist of withdrawal of love or attention. This contradicts unconditional love. The consequence should be chosen carefully and should not run the risk of traumatizing a highly sensitive child. In her book "The Highly Sensitive Child", Dr. Elaine Aron explains that highly sensitive children in particular respond better to positive wording than to punishments or threats. She uses the example of "If you don't go to bed straight away, there will be no more bedtime story!" and rephrases it as follows: "If you come now, we'll still have time for a story!". If you apply this to more than just this situation, you can create a more harmonious family life without threats and with few punishments. Here, too, you can see that the right communication can be the key.

Try to explain to your child what is going on inside them and why they may also find it more difficult to make contact with other children. Children sense that they are different and cannot understand why other children find it so easy to deal with their challenges. In toddlerhood, you can act as a bridge between your child and other children. Establish a connection to make this big inhibition threshold a little smaller, because this interaction with peers is enormously important and valuable. Integration into a group of peers creates acceptance as well as a sense of belonging.

In kindergarten or at school, the most important thing is probably to have the first experiences without the parents. Even if it is particularly difficult for parents to let go, it is essential to allow children to experience things for themselves and develop a wide range of skills. When it comes to new, unfamiliar situations, prepare your child well. Explain what you know about them or do some research together. Go through easy scenarios of what could happen (no bad scenarios!). Perhaps you can take a walk around the outside of the new school beforehand and consider whether a friend from the kindergarten will be joining the class. Be there, pick up on the emotions and discuss them. At the same time, you can think together about what new situations your child has already mastered. If a new situation arises, it is good if all other rituals and structures remain unchanged and only this one situation changes in order to prevent possible overwhelm.

In general, it makes sense to encourage your child to think freely and creatively. Let your child suggest what they would like to do. This way you can practise together how to make new situations less frightening. It's best if your child comes up with the ideas and you support them in the process. This will come gradually, but the journey is the reward. Always stay in contact.

IT'S ALL IN THE MIX - WHY A STABLE DAILY STRUCTURE IS IMPORTANT, BUT NOT ALWAYS RIGHT

There is often a fine line between rules, a fixed daily structure and self-determination for the child. There are many advantages for both sides. That's why, at first glance, they seem to be mutually exclusive. But you can combine them or simply find a good mix.

Structures are important for all children. Fixed rules and a daily structure offer the child a sense of security. They know exactly what is coming and don't need to be afraid of the unknown. It offers them space to try things out and find themselves. This security is even more important for highly sensitive children. Many things in everyday life lead to excessive demands and overstimulation, they have to constantly adapt to new things and always perceive many more stimuli than a normally sensitive child.

A regular daily routine, which usually exists anyway due to work and daycare, etc., is half the battle. Regular rituals and jointly established rules can be a nice addition to this. Give your child their own tasks that are appropriate for their age and do not overtax them. This will boost their self-confidence enormously. You can make it his/her job and give him/her responsibility.

Despite the regulated daily routine and rules, it is important to create enough space for individuality and retreat for everyone.

It is probably best to draw up a daily schedule together, where everyone can express their needs and wishes. Together as a family, we can then decide which wishes can be incorporated and how the daily routine should be organized. Everyone then also has the feeling that they can have a say and experience a certain degree of self-efficacy. They realize that they are listened to when they express their wishes and that these are also important. By expressing their needs, they can influence their situation.

Not everything should be planned, especially at the weekend. Especially here, there should be enough time for family rest and for each family member individually. If special things are planned, such as excursions, meetings with other families, etc., try to ensure the same meal and rest times. These days can also be planned together. Discussing possible challenges can also help to prepare for them. However, you should make sure that you don't present any horror scenarios, but address the emotions that may be imminent and think about how to deal with them.

If you notice in everyday life that you have planned one item too many and your child is overwhelmed, consider whether the situation allows you to replace the item with relaxation. This can also be on a normal day and a completely normal regular item on your schedule. However, every day is different and we all don't always feel the same. Try to act according to the situation if you can.

PREVENTING OVERSTIMULATION AND CREATING SPACES FOR RE-LAXATION

People with high sensitivity experience their emotions, their entire emotional life, particularly strongly. This can be very stressful. Emotions accompany us throughout our everyday lives. Every action is linked to an emotion or triggers one. One day this can be bearable and another day it can be a reason for overstimulation, an excessive demand.

Children in particular learn something new every day. That alone can be exhausting. Add to this a lot of stimuli with extreme emotions, and it can lead even more quickly to excessive demands. We all sometimes feel overwhelmed or overwhelmed by our emotions. However, highly sensitive people experience this state much earlier. Times should therefore be planned in the daily routine that can be used for relaxation and rest.

Because we cannot always influence situations of overstimulation, it is important to deal with emotional tension in calm moments and to develop strategies together. Strategies that serve to relax in order to prevent such overstimulation. They need to be tried out and practiced; it is very likely that they will not work the first time.

Work on these strategies together in a playful way. For younger children, for example, you can build a small cave that is solely for the child to retreat to. Imaginary journeys can also contribute to relaxation.

But how do I even recognize overexcitement? The boundary is usually fluid and not always clearly recognizable, and it can be different every day. Does your child no longer respond to you, does it avoid your gaze? Do you have the feeling that their reactions don't fit the situation, such as screaming, crying, biting, etc.? Other signs may be of a physical nature, such as trembling all over, sweating or dizziness. Your child may be experiencing a flood of thoughts and extreme emotions. In this case, try to take your child out of the situation and give them reassurance by holding them close to your body, if they allow this. Show them that you are there and that they don't have to go through this alone. Speak slowly and in a calming tone. Take note of whether your child is actually listening to you at that moment, otherwise just hold it. Rooms with subdued lighting or nature also have a calming effect here. Children first have to learn how to deal with emotions and even more so with such extreme feelings. The child feels powerless and at the mercy of their feelings. Always give them the feeling that you understand them. This conveys appreciation.

If you often feel powerless in these situations, this is a sign that you should seek support. You don't have to torture yourself, you can make life easier for yourself. And the child notices when the parents are overwhelmed.

To prevent this overexcitement, pay attention to the warning signs of overexcitement. You know your child and are best placed to recognize changes.

Also attach importance to mindfulness and quality in your diet. The blood sugar level should remain constant, which is especially possible with a wholesome, healthy diet. Avoid lots of sweets, especially in the evening. So that your child can concentrate well, he or she should eat breakfast and stick to regular mealtimes. Extreme hunger can also lead to overeating.

When planning your daily routine together, make sure that your child sleeps in a media-free room, preferably darkened. In general, media consumption should be kept as low as possible throughout the day. Televisions, computers, radios and, above all, cell phones are particularly stimulating.

In your living environment, it can also help if you design it with relatively few stimuli, i.e. use few decorations and earthy colors.

Work regularly on allowing emotions and thoughts to arise and addressing them so that they do not become a taboo subject. They should never be the focus of the day, but they should be acknowledged. Give your child the feeling that what they are feeling is okay and also talk about your feelings. Always offer to talk about them, but don't create any pressure.

Professional support may be necessary to talk about the emotions and strategies. It is then also possible to deal with these strong emotions better in the long term.

American scientists have discovered that highly sensitive children are more resilient and less prone to excessive demands if they have spent time with an attentive caregiver in advance, which is due to the release of stress hormones. The chemical messenger cortisol ensures that you as a parent, for example, can hold out for your child even during very stressful phases. Especially when you think back to the many sleepless nights, you sometimes wonder in retrospect how you managed it. However, an increased cortisol concentration over a longer period of time is not healthy. Long-term sleep deprivation or a perspective that no longer has our needs as parents in focus, but only those of the children, must be recognized. Highly sensitive people also reach this state with elevated values much more quickly. The best way to lower the value is with deep sleep, forest bathing, rest, cuddling or creative activities.

WHY ASKING FOR SUPPORT IN NO WAY SHOWS WEAKNESS

Raising a highly sensitive child is an incredible challenge. Do you feel like you can't do it alone? You don't have to. Realize that you are doing a great job every day! Don't be ashamed of it or even feel like you're failing if you ask for support. We all reach our limits from time to time, regardless of the context. It's actually normal that we can't do everything.

And in many areas it is also normal and easy to ask for help. After all, if you're stuck with manual tasks, you can call an expert without feeling like you're failing. And even if you're super good at parenting, it's absolutely fine to get support or ask an expert for advice, because the craft example has one advantage: it doesn't involve emotionally charged situations where I always have to give a bit of myself to achieve something. See your child as a "special task" and not as a punishment if it seems a little more difficult. After all, that's what support is for. If many parents didn't need this, there would be no counseling services etc.

For some situations, it is enough to get some inspiration from a guide or some courage from a trusted person. Sometimes, however, this is not enough and then be honest with yourself and your child.

Sometimes all it takes is an uninvolved third party who is not emotionally prejudiced to provide a little help. This often has nothing to do with you or your competence.

Start by seeking support at a low threshold. Think about who you can trust to help you. Online forums and specialist literature can also help you to take the first step and lower your inhibitions. In online forums, you should of course be careful with knowledge that is not scientifically sound, but it can create a form of solidarity and the feeling that you are alone in this situation becomes weaker. Often the mass of tasks and responsibilities is also the main reason for being overwhelmed. You no longer know where your head is and can no longer think clearly. So build up a private network that can support you. This could be grandparents, friends or babysitters. Asking for support and help doesn't always mean that you don't know what to do or need advice. Sometimes it's just too much and we need some time out.

However, low-threshold, private support is often not enough.

In many places, there are non-binding advice centers that are familiar with the topic. Traditional parenting and educational counseling services are also often a good place to go. For longer-term support, especially with regard to psychological stress, therapeutic support would be useful. This support can be for your child, but also for you. Children notice when their parents are overwhelmed or can no longer calm down due to stress. It therefore makes sense to take care of restoring this calm and relaxation. Otherwise it becomes a vicious circle. The child cries and at some point you become stressed and don't know what to do. You pass on the stress and anxiety to your child and they feel alone and perhaps even guilty that you are stressed because of them. This means that the child does not become calmer. In these cases, it would definitely be advisable to involve an uninvolved third party. Occupational therapists can give you tips or help with activities or support options.

Support can also be provided by a consultation in which you are shown options for support in kindergarten or at school. Tips that you can then also apply at the childcare facility. With regard to school, for example, there is also the option of learning at your own pace in a Montessori or Waldorf school. Find out about the options in good time, also with regard to the choice of school. With a bit of luck, you may also have parents in the kindergarten who already have school children and therefore have a wealth of experience. You can also find out about this on internet forums and websites.

When choosing a secondary school, a school with a focus that matches your child's interests is suitable. This does not mean that he or she needs to be given a lot of support, but it is likely that there are children in the class who have similar interests. Above all, this promotes social interaction and class cohesion. It is important that a positive learning environment is created and that your child feels comfortable.

Great projects and initiatives are easy to find. There are now programs that focus on children's individuality. For example, the "Schule im Aufbruch" project, which aims to develop children's potential and promote their innate enthusiasm, is widespread.

There are now many schools that work according to the Montessori pedagogy and they are also widespread. The main aim is for children to learn at their own pace and according to their interests. Above all, they promote the children's own intrinsic motivation and aim to avoid punishments and rewards. The motto is the well-known phrase "Help me to do it myself".

Involve your child in the decision, but don't give them the feeling that they have to make the decision and bear the responsibility for it alone.

PROFESSIONAL SUPPORT OPTIONS

If private support is no longer sufficient or you or your child need new inspiration, don't be afraid to seek professional support.

Experts primarily recommend physical methods that allow you to feel your own body. This could be occupational therapy or body-related psychotherapy, but yoga or shiatsu can also be helpful here. Therapies that are not reduced to language and do not put so much strain on our minds can have a particularly relieving effect. Those affected who have tried shiatsu or similar therapies describe it as a vacation from their own thoughts and emotions, because they can let go of them for a brief moment.

At the same time, these methods convey a way of getting in touch with oneself and one's body more attentively and develop a special kind of self-acceptance that can be perceived as relieving. As the state of relaxation is often difficult to achieve for highly sensitive people, such experiences are very valuable. Despite their pronounced sensitivity, those affected are often not as forgiving and mindful of themselves as they are of others.

The surprising thing is that it is not necessary for the practitioner or therapist to have knowledge of the client's biography or conversation techniques and the person concerned still feels understood. They describe a feeling of "arriving". Highly sensitive people often do not feel understood by other people. Even if they try to illustrate their perception in detail, a normally sensitive person can hardly understand. This is why quite a few attempts at therapy are abandoned after a while. The feeling of being "wrong" or at least "different" from others, and thus the lack of self-acceptance, is often a main reason for attempting therapy. In today's performance-oriented society, there is often no time to consciously perceive emotions and take time for a mindful break. Those affected feel this very early on. The difficult path to self-acceptance can be accompanied by a psychotherapist if necessary. A therapist can also help them to recognize their own high sensitivity as an asset. Their good ability to reflect always supports the work on oneself.

What's wrong with me? - Child-friendly explanations for high sensitivity

To help your child learn to understand themselves and communicate better, it is important to explain to them what high sensitivity means. In this chapter, you will find suggestions on how you can broach the subject with your child. Focus on a positive but realistic view.

"You perceive more impressions than other children. These can be feelings, moods, sounds or even touch, for example. Your superpower is that you perceive many things much more intensely than other children and adults. However, if there is a lot of it at once, you may be in a bad mood and want to withdraw. It's difficult in kindergarten and at school if it's restless all the time because you hear more noises than other children. Even the quiet noises can sometimes distract you. At school, it can help to go to the toilet for a short break or, if you agree this with your teacher, to do a bit of drawing on the side.

If a lot happens in one day, you will be very exhausted in the evening. You can then try out what helps you. Sometimes it can be reading a book or sometimes a walk in the fresh air. It's different for everyone and you can find out for yourself. You may even need to rest the next day. Having superpowers isn't always easy and can sometimes be exhausting. You can always talk to your parents or a trusted person about it and explain how you are feeling. Sometimes you don't want to talk at all, you just want to be held and cuddled. That's okay too.

If you feel that you are getting restless inside, you are welcome to withdraw. We can build a little retreat together that is just for you. You can snuggle up there and recharge your batteries. Your feelings can sometimes be very strong. You can have nice feelings, but also feelings that don't feel good. Nevertheless, all feelings are important and it's okay for them to be there at this moment. Try out whether music or painting can help you to understand your feelings a little better and let them out. We can do this together, but you can also try it out for yourself.

Not everyone knows or understands your superpowers. If you like it and have the strength for it, you can explain it to them. But there will also be people who simply don't want to understand. It's okay if that hurts and upsets you, it would me too. You especially feel how someone else feels and want to help them when they are feeling bad. But remember that not everyone has this superpower and sometimes can't sense how you're feeling.

Do you feel different? Different is not always bad! There are many children and adults who are like you. Besides, you're a normal child and you have a special talent that others can be jealous of. You're great just the way you are and I wouldn't have you any other way!"

There are great videos on the internet if you need further support with the explanation. It can also be helpful to look at children's books together that talk about high sensitivity.

The core message here should also be that the child is okay the way it is and that it experiences unconditional love and acceptance. This not only lays the foundation for your relationship, but also for your child's relationship with themselves.

INTERACTION WITH OTHER CHILDREN

Especially in childhood, children try to compare themselves and learn by imitation. They may notice that other children don't cry as much or that new things are easier for them.

Highly sensitive children often have the feeling that they are not okay and feel ashamed because they are different. Sometimes all the hustle and bustle in the playground or in the group is too much for them and they withdraw. Occasionally they become loners, although interaction within a group with peers is extremely important in childhood and adolescence. So, if possible, try to act as a bridge between your child and the other children or their parents at the beginning in order to establish contact. For example, suggest playing together to get to know each other in a quieter environment.

Your child not only needs encouragement from you as parents, but also from their peers. Think back to your teenage years. Did you want to spend a lot of time with your parents and did you share your typical "teenage problems" with them? Everyone wants a best friend, an ally in the big, wide world that can sometimes be quite scary.

So if friends have been made, strengthen contact without always being there as the child gets older. This strengthens their sense of autonomy, self-efficacy and, above all, their social skills. By trusting your child to do such small things on their own, you can also strengthen their ability to cope with new situations. So also offer new activities and possible hobbies. Role-playing games are particularly suitable for young children to help them imagine themselves in a safe world that they have created. In this world, they can try out new situations in a safe environment. This may also make it easier for them to come into contact with other children.

As these situations are also new for your child and are likely to make them feel insecure, try to prepare them well again and go through possible scenarios or even try them out in role play.

Dr. Ted Zeff, an American author, has found that it can be very helpful if a highly sensitive child participates in a team sport. A sports team often creates a strong bond and people are committed to each other. So if your child wants to try out different sports, support them. The physical regulation of tension and a feeling of solidarity within the team can be real "game changers".

For interaction with other children, it can also make sense to prepare together with children's books.

10 steps to more mindful interaction with myself and my highly sensitive child

1. Unconditional love and acceptance

See unconditional love and acceptance as the basis for your good relationship with your child and within your family. It should help you to build trust and strengthen your child's self-esteem. It signals "I am worthy of being loved unconditionally". Your basic attitude should be that your child doesn't have to do or achieve anything for you to genuinely love and accept them. You don't have to earn love! It should be the fundamental basis for a trusting relationship.

Think about how you were treated as a child or how you wish you had been treated. What would you do differently or the same? Did you have the feeling that you had to perform well at school and in education in order to receive positive attention and appreciation? Or maybe it didn't even matter what kind of attention it would have been? Remember that a child knows exactly how to get attention. They may not do this consciously, but their subconscious will demand it. However, this often happens through negative attention, because if I behave in the right way, mom will definitely react, even if it's scolding. Then she has eyes for me.

So try to prevent this and approach your child with unconditional love and give them attention so that they don't have to fight for it.

With this unconditional acceptance, you are also showing your child that they have a high self-esteem and are learning to take care of themselves and treat themselves well.

2. Appreciative communication

With appreciative and benevolent communication, we can build on unconditional love and acceptance. Offer your child regular space to communicate with you. However, this should be an offer that takes place without pressure, otherwise it will probably not be taken up. With a trusting relationship, however, you can create a basis for your child to take up this offer and appreciate it.

The best way to signal that you are listening to your child is to integrate active listening. With a little practice, it comes naturally, even in everyday life. It always gives the other person the feeling that we are actually interested and are not asking how they are doing out of politeness. Highly sensitive children sense this even more quickly. In our everyday lives, between all our "to-dos", we sometimes don't have the time or nerves for a detailed discussion. And even if we do take the time and are really interested, it sometimes doesn't come across in this form. Try out active listening and see what you personally can do.

Use I-messages instead of you-messages and, above all, instead of scolding. Explain to your child how you feel and what is going on inside you. Feelings are not a taboo subject, they are part of our everyday lives. With highly sensitive children in particular, it is important to show that everyone has these feelings and that they experience them more extremely or in other situations. But there is nothing wrong with feelings!

3. Psychoeducation for parents and child

In order to learn how to deal better with your own emotions, but also with those of others, it is important to know what is happening in the body. It is worth taking a closer look and trying to understand why something happens and how. You can already find a child-friendly explanation in this book. However, you are welcome to try to find your own explanation in your own words. Perhaps an older child can also explain what is difficult for them or why it is sometimes stressful. Following a crisis situation, you can also reflect together and talk again about the emotions involved. It is important that feelings are not seen as a taboo subject, but that they are talked about openly. Because regardless of whether we address them or not, they are there.

For us as parents, knowledge about high sensitivity offers the opportunity to better understand our children. It can help to reduce the despair we feel because we feel powerless and helpless, because we can accept it better. We also learn a lot about our emotions and how to deal with them.

The children can also understand each other better and learn to accept each other. If they understand that they can't help their peculiarities, this can prevent feelings of guilt. When interacting with other children, they may even be able to explain why they sometimes react differently. So feel free to involve the children at nursery or school if that is okay with your child. However, make sure that you do not unintentionally expose your child.

4. Strengthening self-esteem by promoting skills and independence

As highly sensitive children often have low self-esteem, you should try to strengthen this as early as possible in everyday life. This does not mean that they should be praised excessively for everything, but that you should trust them and have confidence in their ability to do things independently.

Give your child age-appropriate tasks for which he or she is solely responsible (e.g. setting the table, feeding the pet, etc.). Investing the time at the beginning can be a win-win situation for both sides. It frees up a little more time for you and, above all, one less to-do and your child learns to take responsibility and is proud of their own task.

By developing your own interests, you not only promote your child's skills, but also their self-esteem. Encourage your child to try things out and pursue a hobby. Your child should be able to let off steam here, whether physically, mentally or creatively. The activities that allow your child to switch off and relax are individual. Try not to compare or exert pressure.

5. Superpower angle

First of all, our children only learn from us, they learn by imitation. For children, the reality and truth is what their parents tell them. That's why the perspective on high sensitivity is so important. You can have an incredible amount of influence on how you see the world and, above all, how you see your child's characteristics.

There are also great books or videos on the internet about high sensitivity that present it in a child-friendly way. One perspective in particular has stuck in my mind: Treating them as superpowers shows that they are great traits. But even a hero with superpowers needs downtime and spaces to catch their breath. So shape your children's view of the world, but especially their view of their high sensitivity. This can also be done through role play, which the children can also play in kindergarten. Children can better process what they feel and absorb in their own world.

Speaking of superpowers: your superpower is raising your child! It's not always easy and we all reach our limits. But we do our best every day and our children feel that. And when we look at our children, we see the reason why it's worth fighting day after day. After all, we want our children to become strong adults who know their superpower and their self-worth.

6. Providing security through structure and consistency

Create security through a regular daily structure. Create a daily schedule together in a fun way. There are great ways to make a plan or buy a template online. The child can create their own appointments for the day or draw them and stick them on the overview. Hang the schedule in a central place where it can be viewed.

This way, the child can also look at the plan independently and recognize what is coming next thanks to the pictorial representation. Through shared rituals (e.g. reading a book together before bedtime), you create a bond within the family and a stable, safe environment for your child. The organization of the daily schedule could also become a regular ritual. For example, everyone could talk about their day at dinner and then discuss and plan the next day. Be aware of your child's limits here too, so that it doesn't become too much.

Remember that consistency makes everyday life easier in the long term and that a clear line in parenting also gives the child stability. Even if it is sometimes hard and not easy, consistency pays off. However, you know your child best and can sense when it is appropriate to make an exception. When we think back to our childhood, we often remember the wonderful exceptions that were usually only so special because they were exceptions.

7. More mindfulness in everyday life and regular time-outs

High sensitivity can be stressful for everyone, including the whole family. Take time out to recharge your batteries. This applies to your child and also to you as parents. Plan these time-outs in your diary and daily or weekly schedule.

You need relaxation just as much as your child does. They need a clear head at all times and that's not possible when you're under constant stress. So when your child is asleep, take a little time out. Otherwise, if you use the time for household chores, you will still be under pressure and your child will wake up and you won't be able to recharge your batteries.

Try out things that can relax you even at short notice. If you only have half an hour, some things may not be worthwhile or cause even more stress. But perhaps you could do a short meditation with positive affirmations. Look for methods that you can easily implement in your everyday life and start slowly. Don't put yourself under pressure here too, but be grateful for the time out you took today. It's always okay to do what you can today. You want to do this to do something good for yourself and not to create more stress.

Perhaps try meditation or a morning ritual or positive affirmations for a more mindful start to the day without stress. Especially if you are not happy with yourself and doubt whether you are doing a good job, it can be helpful to start the day with positive affirmations or guided meditations. Some people find yoga particularly helpful in the morning to get the right momentum for the day, or in the evening to relax and

switch off. A simple morning ritual can be to drink y-
our first coffee alone and only then wake your child.
Try out new things and give them a chance.

8. Taking a breather in crisis situations

You don't always have to react correctly, nor can you.
In a crisis situation, our reaction is usually strongly in-
fluenced by our emotions. Once the situation is over,
we sometimes regret not having thought about it beforehand. Often the first impulse of our anger is to get
louder or even scream. So if your child is doing something that makes you extremely angry, try to remove
yourself from the situation.

Go into another room for a moment, close your
eyes and take a few deep breaths. Always remember
that your child doesn't want to make you angry and
usually doesn't even consciously want to upset you.
Even if they feel the impulse to make you angry, there
is a reason for it and there is a need behind it. This need
is often attention. At this moment, realize that your
child doesn't mean it personally against you, but that
it is expressing a need and may not yet be able to express it in any other way. In order to be able to express
this need, you first have to be aware of it yourself, and
this is not easy and requires a lot of mindfulness and

practice. So try to understand your child in the moment and take a deep breath. With a clearer head, you will react less impulsively and avoid escalation.

This will not always work, and certainly not at the beginning. In the beginning, try to be aware of the situation and pause for a moment. Give yourself time. Changing behavior in the long term can be difficult.

9. Develop strategies against and in the event of excessive demands

In crisis situations, we are often no longer able to think clearly. That's why it makes sense to think about what strategies could be helpful in these crises when I'm feeling well. There should be a few different ones, because not every one always helps. Every day is different and the degree of overwhelm can also vary. These strategies help us to regulate the intensity, duration and quality of our emotions. The aim is to prevent us from being at the mercy of our own emotions and feeling powerless. Parents are responsible for comforting and helping the child, but later they should be able to do these things themselves. It is therefore important to develop and practise these strategies together.

In his book "Highly Sensitive Men", Tom Falkenstein describes ways of developing strategies that are of course just as useful for women.

- Consciously perceive emotions (What emotions am I feeling at this moment?)
- Be able to recognize triggers (What exactly is the trigger? Is it always in this situation?)
- Acknowledging and accepting emotions (recognizing feelings and enduring them, not acting immediately; it's okay to feel this way)
- Valuing emotions as something normal (Everyone has feelings, it's okay to feel this way.)
- Recognizing the connection between basic emotional needs and emotions (I feel ... because I need ...)
- Self-support (having compassion for yourself; imagination: How would I talk to a friend?)
- Self-soothing (finding alternative, calming thoughts "Everything will be fine")
- Concrete behavioral changes in the situation (consciously doing something differently; change to improve the situation)
- Use of physical relaxation (conscious muscle relaxation; breathing exercises)
- Imagination (fantasy journeys; visualizing resources).

When developing strategies, it is important that your child is in charge and can decide whether to help him or not. In this case, you can also signal to him that you trust him and that he cannot make the wrong decision because he is the professional for his body. Offer to help with the process, but again, this is a voluntary offer that can be declined.

10. Looking for support options

Feel inside yourself and try out what offers you support in everyday life. Build up a network, both in your private environment with friends and in a professional environment with support options from specialists. It's okay to look for support, you can make things easier for yourself. Ask the parents of a kindergarten friend if your child can play with them this afternoon. You could offer the same in return. And then take the day for yourself and recharge your batteries. Babysitters are also often a good way to take regular time out or do things in peace and quiet and thus take some of the stress away. If you need support or an exchange of ideas, find out about like-minded people on internet forums. However, you should make sure that the forums and websites have positive content and do not influence or burden you negatively. Get mental support here or from good friends.

Professional support in the form of therapeutic services can be both long-term and short-term. However, professional advice or just confirmation from specialists that you are doing everything right can also make things easier. You are welcome to seek out counseling centers for this.